# Talking with God

*Prayers and activities based on the Lord's Prayer*

Text by Sarah Knights Johnson
Illustrations by Ron Wheeler

CHRISTIAN FOCUS

© 1998 Sarah Knights Johnson
ISBN 1-85792-232-8

Published in 1998 by
Christian Focus Publications Ltd.
Geanies House, Fearn,
Ross-shire, IV20 ITW, Scotland.

Reprinted in, 1998

Scriptures quoted from the
Good News Bible published by
The Bible Societies / Harper Collins
Publishers Ltd., UK © American
Bible Society 1966, 1971, 1976
used with permission.

Printed by The Cromwell Press.

# Contents

## What's this all about?

In the following pages, you will find the Lord's Prayer taken step by step. Within each phrase, are a number of sections. Each section aims to help you, as a parent or leader of a children's group, to talk to God with your children imaginatively, with relevance and enjoyment.

In this way, children will gain a better understanding of the Lord's Prayer, so that rather than simply reciting it, it may be used as a springboard to further prayer. It is anticipated that where necessary, parents and leaders will adapt the suggestions given to meet the needs of their children.

## How to use this book

Use the contents list to find a section that is relevant to your thoughts, needs or situation.

*Look out for these picture codes as you explore each section.*

A prayer to be read out.

Ideas for discussion, sometimes leading to prayer.

Ideas involving activity, leading to prayer.

Pick one or two prayers
to be read out.

Using Bible verses in prayer.

Bible verses that give ideas
for prayer.

Sometimes it is helpful to find a seat or place that you are comfortable in, to shut your eyes and put your hands together. Then you are able to think about talking to God, your Heavenly Father.

Sometimes it is good to use your hands, eyes and whole body to help you talk to God - just as you would talk to a friend.

# The Lord's Prayer

The Bible tells us that Jesus talked to God often. He helped his friends to talk to God too. He gave them a special prayer to show them how to pray. We call this, the Lord's Prayer.

*We can use this prayer to talk to God too.*

**O**ur Father in heaven:

May your holy name be honoured;

may your Kingdom come;

may your will be done on earth

as it is in heaven.

Give us today the food we need.

Forgive us the wrongs we have done,

as we forgive the wrongs that

others have done to us.

Do not bring us to hard testing,

but keep us safe from the Evil One.

For the kingdom, the power and the glory

are yours, now and forever,

Amen.

*Matthew 6:9-13*

*(Text from the Good News Bible)*

## Our Father in heaven:

**Our Father in heaven:**
May your holy name be honoured;
may your Kingdom come;
may your will be done on earth
as it is in heaven.
Give us today the food we need.
Forgive us the wrongs we have done,
as we forgive the wrongs that
others have done to us.
Do not bring us to hard testing,
but keep us safe from the Evil One.
For the kingdom, the power and the glory
are yours, now and forever,
Amen.
*Matthew 6:9-13*

Dear Heavenly Father,
Thank you that you're the best
Dad in the world. I'm so glad
to be your child.
Amen.

... thank you that you
listen to me because
I'm part of your family.
Amen.

... you know me so well
because you made me.
It's good to know that you
know so much about me.
Amen.

...thank you that you are my
Father in heaven and that I
never have to say, 'Goodbye.'
Thank you that you are always
with me.
Amen.

Copy out one of these
prayers and put it up
somewhere that you'll
see each day.

10

Jesus told us this story to show us how much God, our Father, loves us.

A man had two sons. One day the youngest son asked for his share of the family money. His father gave it to him and off he went.

Soon he had spent all his money on food and drink and wild parties.

Sad and alone, he had to find work feeding pigs. 'I'm so hungry I could eat the pig food,' he said. 'Even my father's servants have more to eat.'

'I shall go home and tell my father that I am very sorry,' he said.

You can find this story in the Bible in Luke 15: 11-24

As the younger son came closer to home, his father saw him. He rushed out and hugged and kissed him.

The son expected his father to be angry, but the father was overjoyed that his son had come home! He told his servants to prepare a feast to celebrate.

11

Find out what Jesus wants us to learn from this story. Choose the right words from the heart shapes to fill the gaps.

sorry

son

close

glad

loves

The father is like G _ _ . He l _ _ _ _ us very much but lets us c _ _ _ _ _ what we want to do, like the s _ _ in the story. Even if we f _ _ _ _ _ about him, God is always r _ _ _ _ to w _ _ _ _ _ _ us b _ _ _ to him. He is g _ _ _ if we say s _ _ _ _ and want to be c _ _ _ _ to him again.

welcome

ready

back

forget

choose

God

12

*Dear Jesus,*
*Thank you for showing us that*
*God is our Father. Thank you that he*
*loves us so much. Help me to love*
*him more and more.*
*Amen.*

# Talk about it

Is there anything else from this story
that helps you to understand what God,
our Father, is like?
Thank God for what you have understood.

Our Father in heaven:
**May your holy name be honoured;**
may your Kingdom come;
may your will be done on earth
as it is in heaven.
Give us today the food we need.
Forgive us the wrongs we have done,
as we forgive the wrongs that
others have done to us.
Do not bring us to hard testing,
but keep us safe from the Evil One.
For the kingdom, the power and the glory
are yours, now and forever,
Amen.
Matthew 6:9-13

## May your holy name be honoured;

Let's take God's name and find words beginning with the letter in His name to show how special He is.

Hello God!
My name is ....................................................
There are other people with my first name but I've not met anyone else called GOD.
Your name is holy.  It is a special name for a special person.

 **G** is for

**God** and also

for **good**

*Dear God,*
*You are so good*
*and you give me*
*so many good*
*things. Thank you.*
*Amen.*

 **o** is for

the **one**

and **only**

*You're so special, God.*
*There is no one else like*
*you in the whole world.*
*I love you, God.*
*Amen.*

**d** is for

all the things

God can **do**

*Lord God,*
*you do the most*
*wonderful things.*
*Praise your name.*
*Amen.*

Can you think of some things God has done that show how special He is? Say thanks to God for these things in a few words like:

*Dear God,*
*thank you that the world*
*you made is so beautiful.*
*Amen.*

*I thank you, God,*
*that even though you are*
*so special, you are still*
*interested in me.*
*Amen.*

*Thank you, God,*
*that you loved the world*
*so much that you sent Jesus to*
*die for us so that we can become*
*friends with you.*
*Amen.*

15

*We give thanks to you, O God,*
*we give thanks to you!*
*We proclaim how great*
*you are and tell of the*
*wonderful things*
*you have done.*

*Psalm 75:1*

When you honour someone,
you tell them how special they are.
Here's a prayer to help you to
keep God's name special.

*You are special, Lord God.*
*You are very special to me.*
*Help me not to use your name*
*in the wrong way at home,*
*at school, wherever I am, because*
*I love you.*
*Amen.*

## Just for fun!

See if you can find words
beginning with the letters
in your name that describe
the way God has made you.

# Play & Pray

## for groups & families

### Where's the prayer?

Write down or draw a picture of several places, people or things that you can pray for. Hide the prayers around the room and let the group or family find them. Talk through how to pray for each topic and spend some time together praying about each need.

Another option is to write a prayer promise on a piece of paper eg: Psalm 116v1 and cut up the paper like a jigsaw with a word on each piece. These words are then scattered around the room and a race begins to see how quickly the jigsaw can be assembled.

### Share a prayer

In small groups or in the family, share something that you would like to pray or give thanks for. Ask everyone to write their names on a piece of paper. Fold and put into a pot or basket. Each person should then pick out a name and pray about the request that that person made.

### Say a prayer

Wrap up a, 'pass the parcel', putting a short prayer in each layer. A variety of prayers could be included: thanks, praise, help etc. You may wish to focus on events which are relevant to the season such as Christmas or Easter. When the music stops, check that the child who opens each layer can read and understand the prayer before saying it aloud. The final layer could contain something which could be shared out amongst the group - sweets are a favourite option!

Our Father in heaven:
May your holy name be honoured;
**may your Kingdom come;**
may your will be done on earth
as it is in heaven.
Give us today the food we need.
Forgive us the wrongs we have done,
as we forgive the wrongs that
others have done to us.
Do not bring us to hard testing,
but keep us safe from the Evil One.
For the kingdom, the power and the glory
are yours, now and forever,
Amen.
Matthew 6:9-13

May your Kingdom come;

Use these words and copy the actions to praise the Lord God, our king. Quietly bow to start with and build up to cheerful shouts of praise, as you remember how great God is.

1)

*Thank you, Lord God, that you take an interest in me and everything that happens to me.*
*You are a great King.*

2)

*I love you because you care about the whole world and whatever happens in the whole world.*
*You are a great King.*

3)

*You love what is right and good.*
*You are a great King.*

4)

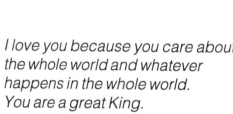

*Thank you that you are able to do more than any other because....*
*You are the greatest King.*

Think of somewhere that you have to go tomorrow or in the coming week.

Perhaps it's somewhere you're really excited about going to, like a club or an outing.

Perhaps it's somewhere that you spend a lot of time, like at school or home.

Perhaps it's somewhere that you're a bit worried about or don't really enjoy going to.

*Why not use this prayer to talk to God about it?*

*Thank you, dear God, that you are my King and that you are with me when I go to ....................*

*.......................................................................................*

*You love what is right and good so help me to do what is right and good when I go there. Thanks for the good things that you make possible there like.............................................................................*

*I know that you will look after me and that nothing can separate me from your love. You are a good and great King.*
*Amen.*

Think of some good news that you have heard this week,
perhaps at school or on television or from your family.
Use this prayer to thank God for the good news.

*Dear God, you are a great king,*
*ruling over all the world.*

*It's great news that*......................................................

...................................................................................

*Thank you that you have made this possible.*
*Amen.*

Have you heard any sad news?
Use this prayer to talk to
God about it.

*Dear God, you are a great king,*
*ruling over all the world.*

*It's so sad that*... .......................................

...................................................................................

*Please give your special help.*
*Amen.*

The Lord is a great king,
ruling over all the world.
*Psalm 47:2*

Can you think of ways you can help someone who is in some difficulty?

Let's thank God for sending Jesus to tell us so much about the Kingdom of God.

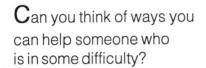

*Dear God, thank you for sending Jesus to show the power of your kingdom in the things he taught, the things he did, and his death and coming to life again.*

*We look forward to Jesus coming again. The power of your kingdom will be shown to be greater than all that is bad and sad in the world now. May many come to know and love you.*
*Amen.*

Our Father in heaven:
May your holy name be honoured;
may your Kingdom come;
**may your will be done on earth
as it is in heaven.**
Give us today the food we need.
Forgive us the wrongs we have done,
as we forgive the wrongs that
others have done to us.
Do not bring us to hard testing,
but keep us safe from the Evil One.
For the kingdom, the power and the glory
are yours, now and forever,
Amen.

Matthew 6:9-13

## May your will be done on earth as it is in heaven.

TO KNOW
GOD'S WILL

*Dear Father, I say, 'I want' so many
times each day. Help me to know
what **you** want - so that I can do
and say what **you** want.
Amen.*

*Lord God, I'm so glad to have
your book, the Bible. It's like a
letter from you to me, telling me
what makes you happy and what
makes you sad. Thank you, Lord.
Amen.*

The Bible is full of messages from God showing us how to live. Choose one and ask God to help you to do what he asks.

Leave all your worries with him because he cares for you.
1 Peter 5:7

Do not steal
Deut. 5:19

And now I give a new commandment: love one another.
John 13:34

Love the Lord your God with all your heart.
Deut.6:5

There are many other messages in the Bible. Ask at your local Christian bookshop or Church bookstall for Bible reading notes to help you understand the Bible.

In the name of our Lord Jesus Christ always give thanks for everything to God our Father.
Eph 5:20

23

*Thank you, dear Father, for a very special person that I can learn about in the Bible - your Son, the Lord Jesus. Everything he did was to please you. Help me to be like Jesus. Amen.*

He was a good friend

He did what God wanted even when it was very hard

He helped people.

He loved everyone

He told others about God

He talked to God

He told the truth

He trusted God

Colour in one of these pictures that show you what Jesus was like. Ask God to help you to be like Jesus in that way today.

Thank God for different parts of your body and ask him to help you use them in ways that he wants. Here are some ideas. Can you think of others?

*Thank you for giving me ears to hear with. Help me to listen to people, when they are happy or sad.*

*Dear Lord, thank you for my eyes to look around. Help me to see all the good things you have given me and be thankful.*

*Lord God, thank you for my mouth and that I can talk. Help me to say nice things even when it's hard.*

*Thank you for my heart. Please fill it with love and care for you, Heavenly Father, and for others.*

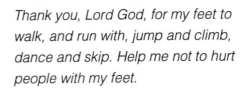

*Dear God, thank you for my hands. Show me how to use them to help others.*

*Thank you, Lord God, for my feet to walk, and run with, jump and climb, dance and skip. Help me not to hurt people with my feet.*

Teach me your ways, O Lord,
make them known to me.
Psalm 25:4

Our Father in heaven:
May your holy name be honoured;
may your Kingdom come;
may your will be done on earth
as it is in heaven.
**Give us today the food we need.**
Forgive us the wrongs we have done,
as we forgive the wrongs that others do to us.
Do not bring us to hard testing,
but keep us safe from the Evil One.
For the kingdom, the power and the glory
are yours, now and forever,
Amen.
Matthew 6:9-13

**Give us today the food we need.**

Lord God, thank you for the farmers,
factory workers, shop keepers and
others who provide my food.
But most of all, I thank you so much
for all that you have given us.

You are the one who made
the land and sea.

You made plants to give grain and fruit.

You give the sun, rain and air to breathe.

You put all kinds of creatures to live in
the water and the air, and all kinds of
animals to live on the land.

I praise you that you have made all
these good things and given them to us
to farm and look after.
Amen.

Thank you, Father God, that you care for the world you have made. Thank you that you go on giving sun and rain and air which help food grow. Help me to care too that everyone has the food they need. Amen.

Lord God, help me not to spoil the land and sea and air with litter and rubbish. Amen.

Heavenly Father, help me not to be greedy so that I can give more to people who are hungry. Amen.

Lord, thank you for the sunshine. It helps things to grow and warms me up! Thank you. Amen.

Thank you that you send the rain to water the plants and trees. Thank you that we have water to drink and use in lots of ways. Amen.

Thank you, Father, for the resources you have put in the earth that we use in our homes like oil, coal, gas, water and things to make electricity. Help us not to waste them. Amen.

Help a grown-up make some food. As you eat it, thank God for the food and how nice it tastes.

Plant a seed or bulb in good soil and look after it. As you see it grow, thank God that he has made it possible for things to grow.

Help a grown-up with the gardening or go for a walk with them in the park. As you enjoy the fresh air, tiny creatures, smells, colours and sounds outside, thank God for the wonderful way he has made the earth.

28

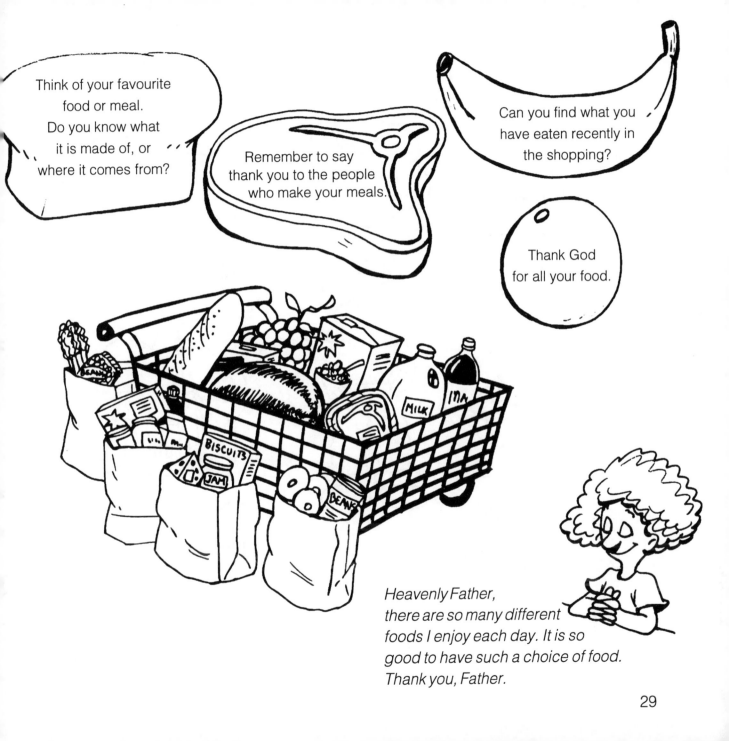

Think of your favourite food or meal. Do you know what it is made of, or where it comes from?

Remember to say thank you to the people who make your meals.

Can you find what you have eaten recently in the shopping?

Thank God for all your food.

*Heavenly Father, there are so many different foods I enjoy each day. It is so good to have such a choice of food. Thank you, Father.*

The food we eat gives us energy and helps our body to grow and stay healthy. We need to grow as a Christian too.
The pictures below show some of the things that help us grow and be strong as Christians.
Can you work out what they are?

*Heavenly Father, I know that I need food so that I can grow and be healthy. Please help me to get the food I need to grow and be strong as a Christian. Amen.*

## Forgive us the wrongs we have done, as we forgive the wrongs that others have done to us.

Our Father in heaven:
May your holy name be honoured;
may your Kingdom come;
may your will be done on earth
as it is in heaven.
Give us today the food we need.
*Forgive us the wrongs we have done,*
*as we forgive the wrongs that*
*others have done to us.*
Do not bring us to hard testing,
but keep us safe from the Evil One.
For the kingdom, the power and the glory
are yours, now and forever,
Amen.
Matthew 6:9-13

I've done something wrong Lord, I'm sorry that I've hurt you and other people by doing things *my* way.

Have you read a part of the Bible recently or heard a Bible story that has shown you some way that you have not done what God wants? Say sorry to God and thank him that he has promised to forgive and love you even if he doesn't like the things that you have done wrong.

But if we confess our sins to God, he will keep his promise......
he will forgive us our sins.
1 John 1:9

31

*Dear Father,*
*I know that sometimes I do or say things that are wrong.*
*I'm sorry Heavenly Father.*
*I know that sometimes I hurt other people's feelings.*
*I know that sometimes I hurt them when I push or fight them.*
*I know that it hurts you when you see me doing things wrong.*
*I am sorry Heavenly Father.*
*Amen.*

Kindness

Patience

Goodness

Jesus showed these things in his life.
Think of something you have done wrong
recently. Was it because you didn't show
one of these good things?

Faithfulness

Peace

Gentleness

Joy

Love

Self-Control

## WHAT CAN YOU DO?

- talk to God about what was wrong

- say sorry

- ask for God's help to put things right

Here are some prayers for when someone has done something to hurt you.

*Heavenly Father, sometimes people do unkind things to me. They make me sad and cross. Please help me to forgive them even when it doesn't seem fair. Amen.*

*Today, Lord, someone upset me. Help me to remember that we all do things wrong. Sometimes I need to be sorry. Sometimes I need to forgive others. Help me to be sorry when I need to be and help me to forgive when I need to. Amen.*

Our Father in heaven:
May your holy name be honoured;
may your Kingdom come;
may your will be done on earth
as it is in heaven.
Give us today the food we need.
Forgive us the wrongs we have done,
as we forgive the wrongs that
others have done to us.
**Do not bring us to hard testing,
but keep us safe from the Evil One.**
For the kingdom, the power and the glory
are yours, now and forever,
Amen.
Matthew 6:9-13

# Do not bring us to hard testing but keep us safe from the Evil One.

How to play:
Choose a counter for each person playing. Take turns to throw the dice and follow the instructions around the track.

The Evil One is also called the devil or Satan. He hates God and tries to stop us from doing what God wants. Turn to the back of the book and you will find a game to play, to show the choices we sometimes have to make between what is right and what is wrong.

Have fun playing it and if you land on the 'On the Spot' squares, see if you can think of some choices you have had to make.

*Heavenly Father, thank you that I know I am safe with you because you love me and care for me. Even when the Evil One tries to make me do things that are wrong, thank you that you are with me and help me to do what is right. Amen.*

For the kingdom,
the power, and
the glory are yours,
now and forever,
Amen.

Our Father in heaven:
May your holy name be honoured;
may your Kingdom come;
may your will be done on earth
as it is in heaven.
Give us today the food we need.
Forgive us the wrongs we have done,
as we forgive the wrongs that
others have done to us.
Do not bring us to hard testing,
but keep us safe from the Evil One.
*For the kingdom, the power and the glory
are yours, now and forever,
Amen.*
Matthew 6:9-13

# Remember to give thanks

At the end of a day, do you like to remember
the good things you've done?
At the end of a prayer, it's a good idea to:

Remember what the
holy God has done,
and give thanks to him.
Psalm 97:12

The end of the Lord's Prayer shows us how to finish
a prayer by remembering what God has done and
giving thanks to him. The words overleaf will give
you some other ideas of how to end your prayers.

For the kingdom,

Thank you, God,
that you care for me.

Thank you God, that
you are my King.

We praise you,
that you are a
powerful God.

the power,

In Jesus'
name, we
pray.

36

You're wonderful, Lord God.

and the glory are yours,

Thank you that you're always with me, Lord.

now and forever,

Amen.

As you want, Lord.

## MAKE A BANNER

Choose a prayer, phrase or Bible verse which has been used in this book to put on a banner. Think of pictures which would help to explain the message.

You will need:

1. **Felt or Cloth**
   Consider where you would like to hang the banner before cutting the size and shape.

2. **Backing materials**
   eg: card / cloth / wallpaper roll cut to size.

3. **Collage materials**

   eg: tissue paper / crayons / paints / wool / textured materials / dry spaghetti / pulses / rice dyed in food colouring / glitter glue / buttons / tin foil / potpourri / wool tassels

4. **Fixtures**
   cane rods / string / plaited wool / ribbons

5. **Fabric glue**
   Please ensure careful adult supervision is given when using glue.

# MAKE A BANNER - If you're stuck for ideas, try this design to help you get started.

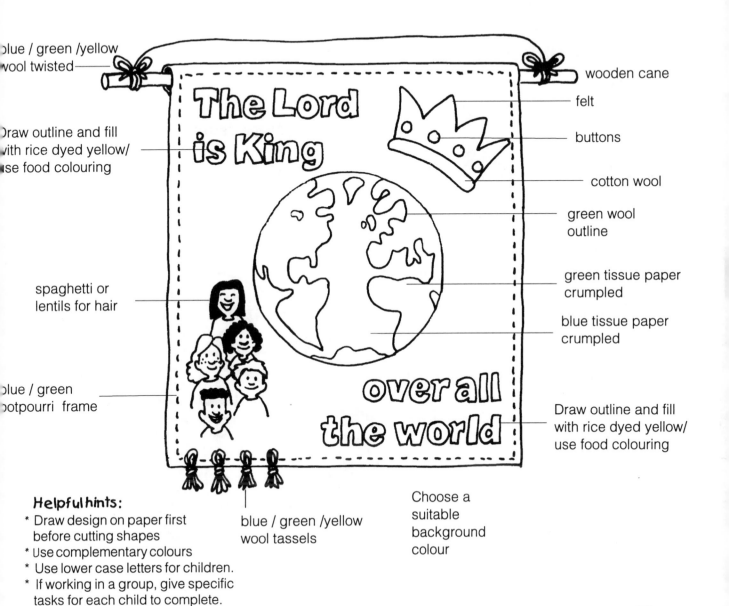

blue / green /yellow wool twisted

Draw outline and fill with rice dyed yellow/ use food colouring

spaghetti or lentils for hair

blue / green potpourri frame

wooden cane

felt

buttons

cotton wool

green wool outline

green tissue paper crumpled

blue tissue paper crumpled

Draw outline and fill with rice dyed yellow/ use food colouring

**Helpful hints:**
* Draw design on paper first before cutting shapes
* Use complementary colours
* Use lower case letters for children.
* If working in a group, give specific tasks for each child to complete.

blue / green /yellow wool tassels

Choose a suitable background colour

# MAKE A Prayer poster

**You will need:**
Large sheet of paper or card,
Small pieces of card,
glue, pens,
paints, crayons,

## Suggested topics:

| | | | |
|---|---|---|---|
| 1 | Family | 6 | School |
| 2 | Friends | 7 | News topic |
| 3 | Church | 8 | Clubs, outings etc |
| 4 | Missionaries | 9 | Say sorry |
| 5 | Home | 0 | Praise |

1. Using card, draw the outline of a telephone, making the poster as big or small as you like.

2. Using the suggested topics given, write these in the squares, using the order shown.

3. Cut out squares to fit over the digit shapes, allowing slightly more card on the left side. Bend the left hand edge to act as a hinge. Apply glue and attach the edge as shown, so that the card becomes a flap. Write the digits on the outside of the flap.

4. Give a child a telephone number, with as many digits as you think appropriate, and let them look under the flaps to find the prayer topics. Discuss with them how to pray imaginatively and specifically for each topic.